S0-BYN-249

LIVING ON THE DRY SIDE OF OREGON:

COMMENTS FROM THE COSMIC COWBOY

by
Keith F. May

Published by:
DRIGH SIGHED
PUBLICATIONS,
PENDLETON, OR

Copyright © 1997
Keith F. May

All rights reserved. No part of this book may be
reproduced in any form, except for the inclusion of
brief quotations in a review, without permission in
writing from the author or publisher.

Published by:
Drigh Sighed Publications
327 SE 1st Street, Suite 131
Pendleton, OR 97801

Photography and illustrations provided by the author
and his darling wife: Christina Rae May

First Edition limited to 300 copies
First Printing • 300 • December 1997

ISBN: 1-57502-648-1

Printed on Recycled Paper

Printed in the USA by

3212 East Highway 30 • Kearney, NE 68847 • 1-800-650-7888

This should be a heck of a lot more fun than chasing tumbleweeds in an Eastern Oregon wind storm. But, if you've never done that - go DO IT before you read any more of this book.

This book is dedicated to those who *have* chased tumbleweeds in wind storms *and* won. Oh, and to my wife and kids, too.

WHICH ONE IS ON THE RIGHT SIDE?
(LITERALLY AND FIGURATIVELY!)

"HOWDY"

"Ah Yes - Eastern Oregon - that idyllic area east of Troutdale somewhere. All the people drive pick-ups and have toothpicks in their mouths - such a quaint slow-paced place." This is the typical thought of a "Valley person".

I'm here to tell you there is more to Eastern Oregon. Some of us have never used a toothpick and actually drive sedans. We who live in Eastern Oregon tend to believe that the Valley people hate us - which is silly - they haven't met all of us yet.

Eastern Oregon is not only a place - but a state of mind. Many people who move here never truly become Eastern Oregonians. And, though they move away, some Eastern Oregonians never actually loose their Eastern Oregonian ways.

This collection of my observations of life in Eastern Oregon covers the years I have lived in The Dalles, Pendleton, Hermiston, and La Grande. Also, as a past resident of Salem, Milwaukee, Oregon City, Portland, and Eugene, I think I can make accurate comparisons between the two regions of the state. (If you don't agree with my comparisons - go write your own book!)

You may want to know why some call me the "Cosmic Cowboy"...The first part comes from a tendency I have to get a little "spacy" at times (like when my wife is asking me to do a chore or when my kids want money.) And the Cowboy part comes from when I was attending the University of Oregon and people found out I was from Eastern Oregon, they jokingly called me a cowboy.

Honestly though, my experience with horses has been limited to watching <u>Mr. Ed</u>, <u>My Friend Flicka</u>, and <u>The Roy Rogers Show</u> on TV as a child. Recently, I thought I'd better gain some actual "horse time", so I got on a four-legged flea bag and took a few trail rides at Wallowa Lake. I didn't know that I could get so chaffed on the inside of my thighs, or that horses don't always act like Mr. Ed, Flicka or Trigger. Cowboys deserve a better reputation, or at least a free can of "Bag Balm".

Surviving life on the "Dry Side" of the state is an art best cultivated with humor, liquid refreshments and truth. If these three items can be kept in balance, you will more than likely survive to tell your grandchildren all about the "good ol' days" before California swallowed up Eastern Oregon. I can help you with the humor and truth parts - the other one is up to you.

OREGON - AS SEEN BY "VALLEY" PEOPLE

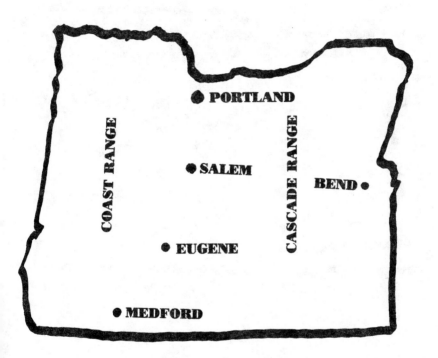

OREGON - AS SEEN BY EASTERN OREGON PEOPLE

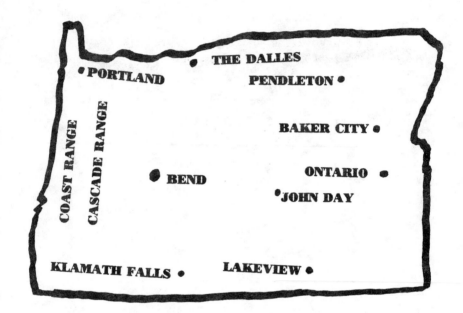

POLITICAL
REGIONS OF OREGON

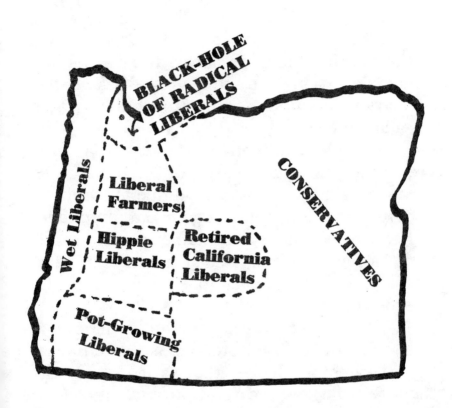

Basically Boogers

Let's talk about snot, your basic boogers. Now, we all know this is a normal bodily function. The body uses this stuff to clean the dirt out that you sniffed up when you were herding the cows across the dusty hills. Snot is also a great place to grow diseases that make you suffer from incredible sinus headaches.

Somehow, snot has gotten a bad reputation over the years. For some unknown reason, rules of proper etiquette prohibit people from digging boogers out in public. (Though, why it is acceptable to blow it out onto a handkerchief, wad it up and put it all back into your pocket to save for later, I'll never know!)

We all know that the only difference between boogers and broccoli is that children won't eat broccoli. Be that as it may, adults tend to be very careful around noses in public. We are all taught not to eat snot, and not to wipe the stuff onto our sleeves. So what do we do about the crusty little boogers? We wait until we get behind the steering wheel of a car, that's what we do!

In the "BIG CITY" people assume auto windshields are specially endowed with a magical quality that makes you invisible to other drivers once you are seated in a car. So, you can pick your nose once you're seated in a car. In the Willamette Valley you see people just mining away in their nose like moles going after a fat, juicy night crawler. And the wonder of it all is that they don't think you see them!

Not so on the dry side of the state. Over here everyone knows that glass is made to see through. You are obliged to look into each car that you pass and make eye contact with the driver. (This is a throw-back to frontier days when you could actually stare down a potential robber. If you happened to glance away it meant certain attack. That's how Billy the Kid got started...no one could really look him in the eye. The snot on his upper lip kept drawing their attention away.)

After a few years in Eastern Oregon you get used to making eye contact with every driver that goes by. The real trick is to see them first, determine if they are friend or foe, and then get "distracted" at just the right moment so that you don't have to acknowledge their presence. Once you get real good at this you can't drive in a big city anymore.

Once, when I was driving in San Francisco, I nearly wrecked the car on Van Ness Avenue trying to look into every car I passed to see if I knew anybody. (I'm almost certain I saw my second cousin, with his boyfriend in a shiny new Sebring convertible.)

So, here we have big city people picking their noses in their cars all over the place, but polite Eastern Oregon people can't actually "do it" when other cars are around. So, when we come to an intersection, we look to see if anyone is coming, and if no one is around, fish a booger out and wipe it on the hem of our jeans. But, if someone is nearby, we have to force ourselves to keep our hands on the steering wheel. The urge to pick is sublimated by stretching and wrinkling the nose in an unlikely attempt to dislodge the booger without the use of a finger. This explains why a lot of strangers to Eastern Oregon see people making funny faces at them, when in reality, we're just being polite and not picking our noses in front of you.

◆ ◆ ◆ ◆ ◆ ◆ ◆ ◆ ◆ ◆

"If the world were a logical place - men would ride side saddle"

Riders in the Sky - The Dalles, OR July 1997

⊕⊕

Eastern Oregon " Nice"

People will tell you that everyone here in Eastern Oregon is soooo "nice". We would never tell you what we really think of you, your ideas or your clothing to your face. About the closest we would come to saying something negative to you would be "Well, that's different!". Beware, this phrase is actually a warning signal that as soon as you leave the room, we will tell everyone what we *really* think.

Most people find it kind of refreshing to visit places like New York City, where the inhabitants tell you what they think in no uncertain terms (and in multiple languages with hand gestures.) But in Eastern Oregon, we all try to be so very polite to people, even though those people are dumb jerks and just crawled out from under a cow pie.

Once, an obvious "tourist" (probably from Beaverton) stopped to ask a rancher if harvesting wheat "took a lot of time." The wheat rancher replied in most polite Eastern

Oregon "Nice" terms that wheat ranching has both good and bad moments, and every job well done takes time. As soon as the tourist was on his way, the rancher turned to his partner and with the strangest look on his face said "well, DUH! Sh__ head"

When you get right down to it "Eastern Oregon Nice" is really code for "passive aggressive".

◆◆◆◆◆

#1 Rule About Eating in Taverns in Eastern Oregon

If the cook or food server have fresh stitches on their head - find the nearest exit.

◆◆◆◆◆
The Library Burned Down!

You know you're from a small town in Eastern Oregon when the library burns down and BOTH books are lost - and one of those wasn't even finished being colored yet!

◆◆◆◆◆
The Tanning Salon

When the first tanning salon opened in Pendleton, all the local hunters brought in their deer hides.

Who Should Run This Country . . .

It really is too bad all the people who know best how to run the country are too busy driving wheat harvest trucks. . .

The Elections and New Year's

Every time the presidential campaign rolls around people begin getting nervous about the T.V. networks reporting East Coast voting results long before the West Coast polls have closed. Someone will complain and then the news reporters all say it doesn't affect the outcome. . . yadda -yadda -yadda.

What I can't figure out is - when New Year's Eve rolls around, the networks delay showing us the ball drop in Times Square until it is midnight on the West Coast.

We can know who the next president is going to be three hours before our polls close, but we have to stay up late to see that stupid ball drop. Go figure?!

Kill That Critter!
or
How to Loose Your Sobriety Every Fall

Hunting is really popular in Eastern Oregon. It must be, because so many people from the Valley come over to do it. I have never figured out why normally intelligent people will spend $80,000 on an R.V. rig, $40,000 on a 4 x 4, $6,000 on guns and ammo, $10,000 on beer and moon pies; all to go spend three days in the cold, damp woods to get 85 pounds of meat that the wife doesn't know how to cook? Why not save all that money and just go buy 85 pounds of meat at the "exotic" meat store . . . try out some alligator or emu for a change.

Actually, I think I know why men from all over the state go hunting. It all goes back to the primal urges men still carry from the hunter and gatherer stages of our development. Waaaay back when, men used to go out and kill animals to feed the folks back at the cave. It showed them that you were a good "provider". The wife's mother would tell her "Ugh, stick with him Debbie, he may be a drunk and a lousy lover, but he is a good provider..."

Men still have these urges to go out to the woods every fall to drink copious amounts of liquid and mark their territory, so they can bring home the meat and prove they're a "good provider". Its a genetic thing, I'm sure.

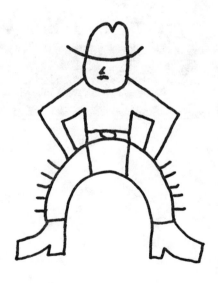

In a store window at Tygh Valley

(If you don't know how to pronounce it or where it
is, you don't get out of the house often enough!)

Most Popular Song in Eastern Oregon in 1975:

"Get Your Tongue Outta My Mouth, 'Cause I'm Kissing You Good-by"

Most Popular Song in Western Oregon in 1975:

Anything by the Grateful Dead

✖✖✖✖✖✖✖✖✖✖✖✖

Most Popular Song in Eastern Oregon in 1995:

"Achy Breaky Heart"

Most Popular Song in Western Oregon in 1995:

Anything by the Grateful Dead

Coffee

Way back when I was younger and old people were *REALLY* old... coffee was coffee.

You'd go into a restaurant and coffee would be listed at the bottom of the menu like this:

coffee, tea, soft drinks

Now, when you go into a restaurant, coffee selections take up a whole page on the menu! Cappucino, latte, espresso, caf, decaf, half-caf, double-caf, veal... it's a whole new language. I'm not sure we really need all of these choices in our life. What ever happened to those simple days when you asked the waitress for coffee and the only thing she said was "cream?".

In the good old "pre-Columbian Roast" days, it was a well known fact in Eastern Oregon that it doesn't take as much water to make coffee as most folks think. It was known locally as "3 to 1 coffee": for every three coffee drinkers you needed one pound of coffee in the pot. It may not have tasted all that great but it sure kept the flies out of the cup.

When visiting friends you could be certain that the polite thing to do was to turn down the coffee offered at least three times before accepting it:

Host "Sooo good to see you folks, won't you have a cup of coffee?"
Guest"No, thanks, we really can't stay long"
Host "But I already have the pot on, its no trouble at all."
Guest"Oh, no thanks, we don't want to be any bother."
Host "I have regular or decafeinated."
Guest"No, really, I shouldn't."
Host "Look, the coffee is three days old, and its really thick!"
Guest"Well.... okay, but don't dirty a clean cup for me."

After this ritual it was acceptable to enjoy your visit and then go home and complain about the lousy coffee.

The good ol' days are gone. Life isn't that simple anymore. After agonizing over the coffee selection at the restaurant your mental capacity is worn out and then the waitress asks you what you want to eat so... to make it simple, you decide on something easy, "turkey sandwich"...

Rye, wheat, pumpernickel, chemical free turkey, ranch run or habitat enhanced white meat, dark meat,? and for condiments...

Trains and Planes

I think I know why we don't have rail service in most of Eastern Oregon...it just ain't fast enough to get anywhere! Once, I was riding Amtrack and it came to a sudden halt somewhere between Arlington and Rufus. I asked the conductor why and he informed me that there was a rattle snake on the tracks. I reminded him that we had stopped five miles back because of a snake as well!

"I know," said the conductor, "but we've caught up to him again."

What we really need is an airline that hits all the major sites -- oops, I mean "lands" at all the major sites. *Dry Air* airlines could serve beer and popcorn as a snack. With flights to Pendleton, Joseph, La Grande, Baker City, Ontario, Lakeview, Klamath Falls, John Day, Prineville, Condon and The Dalles, maybe even with connections to Eastern Washington for those who like to travel abroad. *Dry Air* airlines would help move cowboys to rodeos and toothpick salesmen to their hottest markets. I think their motto could be *It Ain't Your Truck But we Got More Beer.* Anyone got a plane they want to put to work?

❋ ❋ ❋

Living Life by the "Letter" of the Law

The 4 S's of coffee drinking

Sip
Suck
Swirl
Swallow

The 3 C's of basic food needs

Coffee
Chocolate
Coca Cola

The 3 A's of dealing with In-Laws

Step One: Avoid
Step Two: Answer the phone with "IRS-
                   whadya-want?"
Step Three: Arsenic- If the first two don't
                   work.

The difference between In-Laws and Out-Laws

Outlaws are wanted.

The 3 P's of Aging

Puberty
Poverty
Pre-Alzheimer's
(You forget everything after that so it doesn't matter.)

=+=+=+=+=+=

Terrible Truck Accident Claims Two in Eastern Oregon

as reported in the Dayville Daily Drivel
September 5, 1976

"A pickup truck carrying three cowboys went off the bridge and landed in the river yesterday. The driver of the truck was able to get the window down and swim to safety. The two passengers in the bed of the truck drowned. It seems they couldn't get the tailgate down."

Sign in the General Store Window
in Haines, Oregon

Small Town Stuff

My home town in Eastern Oregon is probably a lot like yours. I'm always amazed at the similarities that you can find between the smaller towns of the west. Let's do a little check, put a check mark by all that apply:

___ The police in _(insert the name of your town)_ are so rough, they would frisk a streaker.

___ The name of your local paper should be called: The ____ Minor Gas and Distress.

___ The name of your town sounds like you're telling someone that they have a disease.. (Like: "Aaargh - you've got Elgin all over you!" or "Is that a big fat Hermiston crawling up your leg?"

___ The local Sushi Bar is named "Vern's Bait Shop".

___ The local tanning salon is where all the hunters take their deer hides.

___ Cottage Cheese is found in the "International Foods" section at the grocery store.

___ The main intersection of town has a stop sign...painted on both sides of the sign.

___ When you get an envelope of pictures in the Mail marked "Do Not Bend" your postal clerk writes at the bottom "Yes, they do".

___ The town is so small that the only thing that goes out after ten o'clock is the lights.

___ When you use your blow dryer, the street lights dim.

___ Street maps are printed actual size.

___ The all night cafe closes at six p.m.

❖❖❖

Eastern Oregon Insult #1:

"He's so dumb he couldn't drive nails into a snowbank."

✠✠✠✠✠✠✠✠✠✠✠

There comes a certain time in everyone's life when you discover how much you and your parents are alike... That's a good time to decide that you can love them and/or its time to get counseling.

Scary isn't it?

☽☽☽☽☽☽☽☽☽

Dates and Dating in Eastern Oregon

Dating in Eastern Oregon communities can lead people to believe that celibacy is a viable option. When I was in high school, I knew all of my options very well. (Most of them were named "Debbie".) I had gone to school with them forever. It was very limiting. When I asked someone out for a date they would usually just laugh at me.

Several small high schools in the area used to combine forces to hold their junior/senior prom in an attempt to improve the gene pool for the community. Unfortunately, most of them came from the shallow end of the gene pool to begin with! Contrary to your math teacher, 1 + 1 does not equal 2 when you're talking IQ. You take two people from the shallow end of the gene pool and if they become parents you end up with a child from the gene puddle. . .

My mother tried setting me up with a couple of dates. Grandma thought going to family reunions would be a great way to meet possible future spouse material. When I balked at the idea, they set about suggesting possibilities from among their friends' children.

If Mom told me about a girl that had a "great personality" I knew she probably weighed 275. If Mom mentioned that she had "such a cute face" it was certain that she weighed 350. One time, Grandma even told me to try dating ugly girls so the bullies wouldn't try to kick sand in my face. Gradually, they gave up and let me sort out the girls for myself.

My "First Date"

Each and every first date was a whole new experience for me. It really made me "grow" as a person dating everything from Squeaky Frome to The Wicked Witch of the West. So, when I refer to "my first date", remember, that may really be "my first date...under 200 pounds" or "my first date that didn't try to charge me $50".

MY FIRST DATE used RAID as an antiperspirant.

MY FIRST DATE took one look at my body and said "It's hard to have an X-rated movie with a PG body, isn't it?"

MY FIRST DATE wouldn't kiss me good night after the date but instead left me with these parting words, "Bug off, Bozo!"

MY FIRST DATE was a 38 B, and that was just her shoe size.

MY FIRST DATE told me that there are only two types of people in the world, the bored and the bores. And she was bored...

MY FIRST DATE could actually tailgate herself.

MY FIRST DATE had her hair done at Dunkin Donuts.

MY FIRST DATE'S goal in life was to be able to suck all the cream filling out of a twinkie without the cake collapsing.

MY FIRST DATE had such a dirty mouth, she had to gargle with Pine Sol.

Even the tide wouldn't go out with MY FIRST DATE.

When her pager went off, everyone thought MY FIRST DATE was backing up.

When I asked MY FIRST DATE for her phone number she responded with a 1-900 number.

MY FIRST DATE had only one tooth - but it came in handy for opening beer bottles!

⌘⌘⌘

Actually, all of the girls I've dated (and we're talking way less than five here) were marvellous people. Loving, kind, intelligent, psychotic, and loads of fun...as long as I had money.

My "problem" was that I couldn't date anyone without thinking of them as a potential spouse. I grew up in the era when dating was similar to hunting. You only went into the jungle with the intent of bringing something back to the family.

⌘⌘

We Love it - It's Familiar

We people in Eastern Oregon like familiarity - there is something to be said for landscape that doesn't change for 80 mile stretches, everyone looking the same, and rules of etiquette that go unchallenged for generations. I think the word that best sums it up is - BORING! But then again - boring means predictable - and that means less energy spent trying to figure life out - which means more time to watch the satellite T.V. - which is also kind of familiar and BORING!

At a Cowboy Bar in Prineville the urinal in the men's room has a sign above it that says:

"No wonder you're going home alone"

A sign above the mirror in the women's room says:

"He's not good enough for you!"

Imnaha Store - Men's Restroom Urinal

(Top sign says "Stand Close - its shorter than you think"
Bottom sign says "Objects may seem larger than they appear")

MAD. P.

In Eastern Oregon the Mother's Against Drunk Driving gave up the fight . . .

It seems that some frightening statistics made them realize they were after the **wrong** group of drivers. When they heard that 50% of all accidents were alcohol related, it occurred to them that 50% of all accidents were "sober" related.

So, they formed a new group called Mother's Against Drivers. Period. (MAD.P.) Their first fund raiser involved a chili cook-off at the park, but no one showed . . . everyone stayed home to avoid the sober drivers.

☝ ☝ ☝ ☝

Eastern Oregon Insult #2:

"He's so lazy, molasses wouldn't run down his legs."

Eastern Oregon Drawl

People in Eastern Oregon generally speak slowly. We figure if people talk too fast, their mouth will be saying things that their brains haven't even thought about yet.

If you really want to scare an Eastern Oregonian, just start talking really fast.

WORD OF CAUTION: Don't try this with a State Trooper. They'll assume you're from California and you're high on drugs. They have orders to shoot to kill.

Eastern Oregon Insult #3

He couldn't hit the ground with his hat
in three tries.

#####

You know you're in Eastern Oregon if. . .

- the primary color of most cars is "bondo"

- the rear tires on the cars are twice as wide as the ones on the front.

- the gas cap usually consists of a rag.

- the pickup truck in front of you has
    a) a gun rack WITH guns
    b) a dog in the back of the truck
    c) a bumper sticker that uses four letter words
    d) mud flaps with buxom silver women icons

You Know You're in Western Oregon If. . .

- the primary color of most cars is "earth" tone.

- the back tires and front tires have matching slash marks.

- the gas cap is missing, (so are the hub caps and hood ornament).

- the pick-up truck in front of you has:
  a) out of state plates
  b) a canopy to cover the
     carpeted truck bed.
  c) a bumper sticker for
     McGovern
  d) mud flaps with Yosemite
     Sam or peace symbol

♦♦♦♦♦♦♦♦♦♦♦♦♦

You'd love being out here in Eastern Oregon - there's just nothing doing every minute. In reality, it's only 20 minutes to Portland - by phone.

② ② ② ② ②

Everyone will be better off when they realize
that
Eastern Oregon is the center of the Universe.

⑧ ⑧ ⑧ ⑧ ⑧

"Myths" Eastern Oregonians believe about people who live in the "Valley"

People in the Valley think the distance for you to travel to Salem for a meeting is acceptable, but they would never think of driving from Salem to meet with you because its "just too far". (This is known as the time/distance/dead-butt ratio. Valley people can't travel far or for great lengths of time because they will get a dead-butt. They assume that Eastern Oregonians *CAN* travel far for great lengths of time because we *ENJOY* meeting dead-butts.)

Valley people and beer bottles have two things in common . . . they are both empty from the neck up.

Valley people think that green is the only lawn color option.

Valley people think that one inch of snow equals a holiday.

Valley people actually enjoy all that rain because it is the only time that:

1) the air smells good
2) burglaries decrease
3) street people get a bath.

Valley people think that Eastern Oregon is backwards, quaint, and in need of "fixing". (Eastern Oregon people look at the Valley and see how it was "fixed" and respond with a hearty "HELL NO!")

Valley people don't know that the Wallowas are more than 50 miles east of The Dalles.

Valley people think that Central Oregon *IS* Eastern Oregon. (Actually, much of Central Oregon qualifies for Eastern Oregon Status, but Bend qualifies for California Status. . .)

◆◆◆◆◆◆◆◆◆

Eastern Oregon Insult #4

Your family tree was only a bush.

Sex Ed

Wasn't your High School "hygiene" class a joke? Some old geezer with horn-rimmed glasses and a pocket protector trying to talk about "sex" without ever really saying anything. Even the films never really said anything. Why couldn't they just cut to the chase and tell us all about it?

Grandma always used to say there were other things in life than sex - but she never told us just what those other things were - "There's nothing wrong with sex. It's a perfectly natural, disgusting act." she would say.

I think Disney came out with a movie they showed the girls called "Snow White Gets Her First Period" and for the guys they had "Pinocchio Gets a Woody". But most schools thought that these films were too controversial, so they wouldn't show them.

Most small Eastern Oregon high schools had to save money so they combined drivers ed with sex ed. That way you learned both in the same car ... and the schools had to pay only one teacher ... pretty smart, huh!?

❑ ❑ ❑ ❑ ❑

Eastern Oregon Insult #5

If his I.Q. were ten points higher, he'd qualify as a hammer.

❑ ❑ ❑ ❑ ❑

Sign at the city limits of Joseph

The Work Place

Ever get to work and everyone is in one of those "dark moods"?, just ask them:

"Drink your spit cup by accident this morning?"

Just pray they don't go "postal" on you and blow everyone away...

Word of Caution: Don't try this with the State Trooper when he/she is in a "mood". He/she would assume you're from the Ozarks and don't have an IQ high enough to drive a car, let alone play the banjo. And don't forget, they have orders to shoot to kill.

^ ^ ^ ^ ^ ^

Baccalaureate

Baccalaureate Service = that's when parents realize they haven't taken their kids to a religious service since cousin Fred was married, unless of course you count that Little League baseball game when you and the whole family prayed "I hope the Ump didn't see that".

In Eastern Oregon everyone assumes that everyone else is religious and attends church regularly. (Though statistics show that only about 15% of the population attend a church regularly ... and no, Easter and Christmas services are not counted as bonafide "regular".)

Since everyone assumes that everyone else is going to church this means you can't mow your lawn on Sunday morning for fear of offending the neighbors (This would be Saturday for those living in the Milton-Freewater area ... large population of Seventh Day Adventists there.)

Actually, I think more people would attend church if lottery tickets were available in the Narthex. Also, if preachers would learn that 12 o'clock means "take a vow of silence and let your people GO ~ HOME!" And while we're at it, why not recliners instead of pews, and how about some vendors selling beer nuts and snowcones up and down the aisles during the slow parts of the service? Most men wouldn't mind having a remote control in their hand either...

Toilet Seats and YOU!

Just when will the women of the world learn to leave the seat up? A "Real" woman in Eastern Oregon does her man a favor, and leaves the seat in the up position to save him time during those quick trips to the rest room during TV commercials.

We all know it takes the average man 80 seconds to do his job in the bathroom, while women, on the other hand, take an average of two minutes and 40 seconds. Women take THREE times as long . . . so, while they're in there, they have the time to put the seat back up. Men, on the other hand, have to rush back to the couch for more important matters.

We are very grateful that most of us in Eastern Oregon now have indoor plumbing. Before indoor plumbing it was really disgusting when the blow dryer fell into the pit - but at least no one was electrocuted. Blow dryers in the toilet bowl account for 99% of the accidental electrocutions of constipated women in Eastern Oregon.

Many years ago we had a fire in our bathroom - we were grateful that it didn't spread to the house.

Actually, men in Eastern Oregon are still trying to figure out why public men's rooms have both sinks *AND* urinals - "What do you need both for?" - is a comment often overheard.

The Family Vacation

The Family Vacation (or "the trip from Hell" as it is known by the guys down at work) is a time-honored tradition in Eastern Oregon. It is almost like an annual migration, like the salmon headed upstream to spawn or like women headed to Nordstroms for the fall fashion show or maybe like the line of cars headed out to garage sales on Saturday mornings in June.

When planning a trip, men never take into account the things that people would want to see ... like say - Disneyland - unless, of course, there is a relative that lives close by that the whole family can move in with for a week - rent free.

If you really wanted to see exotic places - like Paris, Singapore, New York, etc. then that's when you'd refer to your program listing for the PBS travelogue programming or look through some old National Geographic Magazines.

You may not have seen cousin Fred since you were kids and he threw you in the irrigation ditch to see if you could swim, but since he now has a place in Burns, you've always had a hankering to see that part of the country - never mind that the kids had their hearts set on seeing Six Flags over Who Knows Where at $800 a day.

Having relatives to vacation with is almost like a time share. You get a week at cousin Fred's place this year. Next year he drops in on you with his wife, dog and three varmints he calls children for a week because he has always wanted to see Pendleton in August. (I'm sure it's almost as good as Paris in the Fall for Fred.)

As a child, I always looked forward to the "Family Vacation". It meant we got to eat out! Of course, for my family, eating out meant stopping at a grocery store and buying a loaf of white bread, a package of pimento flavored bologna, and a jar of mustard. (And my parents wondered why my brother got carsick everywhere we went?)

As a father, I decided no bologna for my family on trips...we go first class, McDonald's Happy Meals for everyone. They just had to learn how to eat in a moving car and NOT spill anything on the seats or carpet.

Driving long distances with the family car full of screaming children, loaded down with 16 suitcases and a sack of snacks is just *part* of the "Family Vacation". The other part is reaching around behind you trying to swat one of them while still holding onto the steering wheel negotiating traffic in downtown L.A. Not only does this tend to increase your flexibility, your child learns valuable lessons on how to squirm just out of Dad's reach.

I think I have found the solution to screaming, whiny children entangled in backseat brawls: just drop them off alongside the roadway somewhere between Boardman and Arlington on a 109 degree day in August. Let them walk down the road for about three miles. Then, after the Children Services Department lets you have your children back, you're better able to tolerate their joyful screams on long trips out of state.

I have successfully taken my children to Disneyland, Sea World, Yellowstone, Glacier National Park, San Francisco, Aunt Frieda's Farm, Mt. Rushmore and all the tourist sights in between. We did it all in seven days.

I decided to get it all over with and put years of pain into one major "Family Vacation". The male in me needed to "conquer" the road everyday. (Men don't want to stop - that's because they want to walk in to the motel at the end of the day and tell the clerk that they made it there in six hours, 18 minutes and 43 seconds. It's a great way to impress a total stranger.) I'm sure I was running on pure testosterone for the entire seven days.

It was a major challenge to get the wife and kids back into the car to drive 950 miles each day. My children learned valuable lessons on bladder control, sleep deprivation, and 20 minute museum tours. I'm sure they will pass these priceless lessons on to my future grandchildren as well, or spend many sessions in group therapy.

Now, when I mention taking a family vacation, both of my kids plead to go to summer camp at a military school in Africa

My wife, on the other hand, has made it abundantly clear that from now on we see one, and only one, "sight" per vacation. (Such as a large cruise ship headed into the sunset with us on the Lido deck sipping caffeine free diet cokes...)

It's either that or we all go to a nudist camp so we can avoid packing...

Cousin "Fred's" Place in Kent
(Yeah, there IS a Kent - located between
Grass Valley and Shaniko)

Eastern Oregon Insult #6

Both he and his dog use the tree at the
corner.

Parenting

Parents in Eastern Oregon maintain a high standard of parenting...they figure if they do it right their children will feel guilty about EVERYTHING!

Hell and Marriage

Hell holds no fear for those who have been married. When arriving at Hell, the little demon just takes one look at you and says, "uh oh, another married guy, well, you've got a choice of tortures:

a) no sex for eternity (it just seems that way),

b) bad sex for eternity (it just seems that way), or

c) red hot pokers jabbed in your eyes every 30 seconds for eternity.

What'll it be?"

Usually the married guy will take the last one, he's already experienced the other two and is ready for a change of pace.

An Eastern Oregonian died and went to Heaven. St. Peter met him at the gate and asked her where she was from.

She replied "Eastern Oregon."

St. Peter replied "Well, come on in - but you're not going to be satisfied."

Recent Poll of Oregonians

Recently the polling firm of Ronnie Plutz & Co. conducted an extensive sample polling of 17 people in various locations in Eastern Oregon to determine their opinions on various issues. A second version of the poll was then given to 214,945 people in various locations in Western Oregon so comparisons could be made between the two regions. You may wonder why so few Eastern Oregonians were polled - but Ronnie said it really didn't matter because he knew what they would say anyway... Below are the questions and the results:

1a. (Eastern Oregon) Why do you hate people from Western Oregon and despise everything they say and do?
    a) They are all jerks 67%
    b) Is this some kind of test? 14%
    c) That's a loaded question isn't it? 11%
    d) Where's Western Oregon? 8%

1b. (Western Oregon) Why do you suppose that people from Eastern Oregon hate and despise everything you do?
    a) I haven't been to Starbucks yet this morning, back off Bozo. 53%
    c) They need to "center" themselves and try some herbal remedies or, like, try group therapy, maybe. 11%
    d) There is an Eastern side to Oregon? 36%

2a. (Eastern Oregon) Since you are a redneck and have a low IQ, don't you think that Salem is better at deciding what is best for your future?
- a) Those #%@!*'s don't know how to blow their nose, let alone spend my tax dollars. 45%
- b) Is IQ anything like DQ? 15%
- c) Rednecks are funny. 25%
- d) Isn't Salem where the prison and state mental institutions are located? 15%

2b. (Western Oregon) Don't you think Salem is better at managing the natural resources of Eastern Oregon rather than allowing the anti-animal rights, pro-logging, environmental despoilers of Eastern Oregon destroy the vast pristine beauty that all Oregonians have a stake in preserving?
- a) Yes 101%

3a. (Eastern Oregon) Would you describe your political beliefs more like that of the Democratic Party or the low life, scum sucking Republicans, or some other party?
- a) Democratic Party 35%
- b) Republican Party 40%
- c) Independent Party 25%

3b. (Western Oregon) Would you describe your political beliefs like that of the Democratic Party or the low life, scum sucking Republicans, or some other party?*

a) Democratic Party 20%
b) Republican Party 15%
c) Independent Party 17%
d) Cocktail Party 20%
e) Save the Whales and Free Coffee for Everyone Party 18%
f) I wanna do anything I wanna do Party 13%
g) Joggers From Hell Party 7%
h) People for More Freeways and Save the Trees Party 21%
i) Its My Party and I'll Cry If I Want To Party 14%

*note: total is more than 100% probably because most people in Western Oregon don't vote and/or lied.

4a. (Eastern Oregon) Which antiquated, patriarchal, guilt laden religious group would you most likely associate with:

a) Catholic 20%
b) Seventh Day Adventist 20%
c) Mormon 20%
d) Baptist 15%
e) Episcopal 5%
f) Lutheran 5%
g) Various other protestant religions 14%
h) I'd be going straight to Hell if I believed there was such a place 1%

4b. (Western Oregon) Which path of personal enlightenment have you found best suits your personal belief system?

    a) Buddhist 15%
    b) Shamanism 15%
    c) Yoga 15%
    d) Current cult fad 15%
    e) No religion, just good food and plenty of exercise 15%
    f) "Traditional religions" such as Catholic, Judaism, Moslem, and protestant dogmas 15%
    g) Drug Therapy 10%

Conclusion:

    Polls can be manipulative and have predetermined outcomes. Don't ever pay any attention to them.

Car Aerobics

I bought this cassette tape to listen to while I go on long drives in Eastern Oregon: It's called <u>Car Aerobics Your Way to Fitness.</u>

It goes along with some perky music and sounds something like this:

Turn your steering wheel, turn and turn and turn and turn.

Use your wiper blades, wipe and wipe and wipe and wipe.

Visor: up and down, and up and down, and up and down.

(And the most strenuous of activities...) Brake and brake and brake.

Repeat the above for the next 220 miles.

After that strenuous work out, I usually have to pull alongside the road for a "power" nap.

ㅇㅇㅇ

Western Oregonians are so boring - when you ask them how they are doing - they tell you!

◆□◆□◆□◆□◆

Eastern Oregon Holidays that we Add to Our Calendars

June 15th - "Are you SURE I'm the Father?'s - Day"

August 23 - "Absolutely Last Day to Remove your Studded Tire Day"

August 24 - "Put your Studded Tires On Day"

Second Full Week of September - Pendleton Round-Up, put the world aside and be a cowboy for a week

November 1 "Wash the Egg off your Car Day" (day after Halloween)

Western Oregon Holidays

May 8th - " Mow the Moss on Your Roof Day"

August 4th - "Look! That Strange Thing in the Sky is called *THE SUN*" Day

November 12th - "Elk Season in Eastern Oregon - Go Shoot Anything With Four Legs Day"

Eastern Oregon Golf vs Western Oregon Golf

Western Oregon Golfers just ask for three things:
>golf clubs
>reasonable weather
>guaranteed tee time

Eastern Oregon Golfers want:
>golf clubs
>fresh air
>Beautiful sexy golf partner

(Note: if they get the last item - they usually skip the first two.)

✖✖✖✖
My little brother was a mean, vicious child - he would always hit me back!
✖✖✖✖

The Drought

Every few years it seems we go through a drought in Eastern Oregon. (For those of you in Western Oregon - that means we ain't got enough water to keep the fairways green.)

✖During the latest drought the prisoners in the Eastern Oregon Correctional Institution were served just bread and bread.

✖Water was so scarce that when a house caught on fire the firemen had to blow it out.

✖The restaurants had to charge for a glass of water - and a man from Lake Oswego complained because they brought him the wrong year.

✖The fish in the reservoir bought a mobile home.

But then again - not every year has drought conditions, recently we had too much water and the stores were doing a brisk trade selling bottled dust.

Men & Women of Eastern Oregon

Women have noticed these things about men in general in Eastern Oregon:

- 90% of the men give the other 10% a bad name.
- Men marry later in life - and die earlier.
- Most women in Eastern Oregon nick-name their husbands "knickknack" because men do about the same amount of work around the house.

Men have noticed these things about women in general in Eastern Oregon

- Women would rather be right than objective.
- Express an opinion and you'll find out why they're called the opposite sex.
- Women in Eastern Oregon like to wear their hair in pony tails so tight that when they blink their eyes - their mouth pops open.

The Death of the Old Ranch Hand

The ranch hand had worked for years on the ranch and now lay dying on his bunk in the bunkhouse. He called over his old friends to make his final request.

"Boys, fetch me my gun and let me shoot it out the window. Where the bullet lands is where I want to be buried."

So he was given his gun and he fired it. Two days later the old ranch hand passed on. His friends gathered and in accordance with the old man's wish, they buried him on top of the barn.

Death Rate in Eastern Oregon: one per person

Eastern Oregon Insult #7

Your father is as strong as a horse-
just wish he had the IQ of one!

Real Estate Ad From 1967

FOR SALE: 1 bedroom shack on 80 acres. Good hunting, fishing nearby. House needs some work. $12,500 owner will carry contract and help with clean up and repairs

same place after *Californians have arrived in Eastern Oregon:*

FOR SALE: Luxurious mountainside rustic retreat. Master Bedroom with a view of wild and scenic river. 80 acres of timber with Bambi and friends. Near wilderness area. No covenants, or subdividing allowed, perfect weekend get away. $1.5 million - CASH TERMS ONLY

Eastern Oregon Residency

Yes, its true - you too can be a bonafide resident of Eastern Oregon. It may take you some *time* - but if you live in Eastern Oregon - that is the one thing you'll have lots of. Check over the requirements and start working on it. Here is how we label people's residency status:

VISITOR: Lived here less than 20 years

NEWCOMER: Lived here 21 - 60 years

OLDTIMER: Lived here 61 - 90 years

PERMANENT RESIDENT: Those buried in the local cemetery

Some other "rules" that may apply include:

1. If you were born here - but moved away at an early age - you may still be considered an OLDTIMER *if* you have the right last name.

2.   If you lived here for less than five years sometime during the past 80 years, you are entitled to an extensive obituary in the newspaper *if* you have the right last name.

3.   If you have lots of money, own a ranch (you must actually *work* on it), and attend the correct church and lodge - you can buy NEWCOMER status in less than five years.

4.   If your great grandmother came to Eastern Oregon in a covered wagon to work in a brothel, and she had several illegitimate children - their descendants increase in social stature proportionate to the years that pass.

5.   Rodeo Princesses and Queens will *always* be Rodeo Princesses and Queens - it will be a requirement that this title be engraved on their headstones. (Note: A Big Rodeo like the Pendleton Round-Up requires that the first-born female of the princesses and queens must also become royalty - or face a life of ignominy working in a fast food restaurant in Gresham.)

●   Other factors that may alter your residency status:

1.   add 12 years to your residency if you purchase a home on the "correct" side of town.

2.   add 16 years if your son or daughter marries into an OLDTIMER family.

3.   deduct 10 years if you work for the government.

4.   add 25 years if you can ride a horse and drink a case of Budwiser at the same time.

5.   add 30 years if your son is the local high school quarterback - *and* he's really, really good.

6.   deduct all years and plan on moving out of town if your son is the local high school quarterback - *and* he's really, really bad.

7.   add the number of years you have been alive if you were born in Eastern Oregon and moved away before the age of two - but you moved back as an adult. (All years in foreign lands - such as Lane County - are purged from your record if you return "home".)

Gardening in Eastern Oregon:

Notice in this photograph the lovely vegetable and flower garden of Stella Crup of Meacham, Oregon. The luxuriant growth of zucchini, tomatoes, cucumbers are artfully growing amongst the zinnias, asters and hollyhocks. This picture was taken on July 10th - the morning following the annual July blizzard.

Unfortunately, Stella had never suffered through a harsh summer at Meacham before - she currently resides in cell block 9 at the State Mental Institution in Salem...

(She was unaware of the three seasons in Eastern Oregon High Country: Last Winter, This Winter, and Next Winter.)

The Japanese Businessmen

The Japanese have discovered Oregon, of course. They love the beauty of the State and they find the agricultural products perfect for their home markets. Often, the Japanese will send their businessmen to Eastern Oregon to personally negotiate deals for beef, wheat and Hermiston melons.

Recently two Japanese business men arrived in Hermiston to look over the crop of melons. One of them started talking in Japanese but the other interrupted him. He said, "You're in Hermiston, Oregon, part of the USA now. Remember to speak in Spanish!"

EASTERN OREGON PARTY ETIQUETTE

◆Abstinenece from liquor is requested when at a public event - (unless it is the Red Cross Wine And Cheese Tasting Fundraiser...) - if you MUST drink, be sure to share the bottle. Otherwise, the other guests will think you are selfish.

◆Chewing tobacco is always permitted at outdoor events - just remember to spit _with_ the prevailing wind, not against it. At indoor events - chewing tobacco is permitted as long as you can hold onto a spit cup _and_ your beer can and not get the two mixed up.

◆Foul and obscene language is NOT permitted when children and women are present - unless they start using it first.

◆Forbidden topics of conversation: the mating habits of coyotes _and_ your in-laws, cattle vs. sheep wars of the past 150 years, and your latest attempt to outwit the IRS.

◆Firearms are usually permitted at social gatherings. Do not fire them for pleasure or shoot at drunk women unless they deserve it. Be aware that the loud noise from a gun tends to bring the police officers.

◆If you need to use the rest room - remember to loudly announce to all of the guests that you have to go to "Peeee - oria" or for variety announce that you have to go to "Whizzz- consin".

♦When playing card games, remember that the host and hostess prefer that you wipe the orange Cheetos dust onto the napkins, NOT onto the cards, tablecloth, or hunting dog.

♦When the party includes dancing - visit Peoria and Wisconsin frequently if you do not know how to dance.

♦You will know that it is time to leave the party when these three things occur:

1) Your wife kicks you in the shins uncontrollably when you start telling your favorite jokes.

2) The host starts to look "sexy".

3) You notice how lovely the lampshades are - from the inside of one.

The Arrival of Marcus Whitman - Missionary- and his (alleged) first Conversation with the Cayuse Tribe

Marcus and Narcissa Whitman along with the Spauldings had travelled across the plains from the east in 1836 to preach the Christian Gospel to the Indians of what later became Eastern Oregon and Eastern Washington. As they first descended the Blue Mountains, they came to an encampment of Cayuse surrounded by thousands of their beautiful Cayuse ponies.

As the people rushed up to Marcus, he held his hand up to stop them and began to address them.

"I have come from a peaceful land of white people," said the missionary.

And the people shouted out as one, "Sikem tsein!"

"A land where people are free and equal and love one another."

"Sikem tsein!" shouted the people again.

"We have travelled many months to come to you and show you how you can change your lives for the better."

"Sikem tsein!"

"You can give up this miserable nomadic life and be contented and happy like my people."

"Sikem tsein!"

Marcus then noticed the vast herds of horses wandering around on the gentle slopes of the Blue Mountains. "What an interesting breed of horse," he said. "May I have a closer look at them?"

The chief said "Oh sure, go ahead, but be careful not to step in the sikem tsein!"

In Conclusion:

Living on the dry side of Oregon has its ups and downs. (And I'm not just talking about taking a drive out on a county road.) As you have probably already noted, there are many things to remember to avoid social faux pas in Eastern Oregon. And now you know some of them.

As Dr. Livingston (the "I presume" guy) is reported to have said "The key to understanding any primitive society is knowledge of their culture and their eating habits." He said this on his way to being tossed into the stew pot, but it applies to this part of the world as well.

Hopefully, you now have a generous supply of priceless tidbits of information that will help you better understand your life on the Dry Side or (if you are one of those despised "tourist" types from the Wet Side,) you are better prepared to deal with the wild natives.

As with any work of this nature - the names have been changed to protect the innocent AND the guilty. Any resemblance to real persons, places, or events are merely coincidental. All characters are figments of the author's imagination or are merely voices in his head - (they are not - they are too - shut up you guys!) Some people may need to seek counseling with a licensed therapist at this point, and the author is NOT responsible for the cost of treatment. Have a nice day ...

Humor is truth - faster

Keith F. May

Keith F. May is a veteran first grade teacher in Pendleton, Oregon and also an adjunct history instructor for The Heritage Institute of Seattle, Washington. He has taken hundreds of teachers out to explore the Oregon Trail and ghost towns of Eastern Oregon each summer since 1992. Keith was named "Outstanding College Educator of the Year" in 1995 by the Oregon/California Trails Association for his work teaching educators about Western Migration.

Keith was born in Pendleton and moved to The Dalles in 1956. Keith is a graduate of The Dalles High School and the University of Oregon. He and his wife, Christina, have also lived in Hermiston and La Grande before coming home to Pendleton in 1984 which makes Keith an honorary "oldtimer" with plans on becoming a "permanent" resident. (see page 69 . . .)

Keith's other works include:
Ghosts of Times Past: A Roadtrip of Eastern Oregon Ghost Towns
A Field Guide to Historic Pendleton
A Field Guide to Historic The Dalles
A Tour of Pendleton's Historic Homes
*Finding The Trail in Oregon: A Guide to Sites, Museums and
Ruts on the Oregon Trail*

OTHER BOOKS AVAILABLE FROM DRIGH SIGHED PUBLICATIONS.

Ghosts of Times Past: A Roadtrip of Eastern Oregon Ghost Towns (c) 1996 by Keith F. May. A guide to finding ghost towns in North Central Oregon and the gold mining region of the Elkhorn Mountains. 95 pages ISBN 1-57502-107-2 pbk $11.95

A Field Guide to Historic Pendleton (c) 1997 by Keith F. May. Take a look at the origins of this once wild frontier town. Many historic homes and buildings remain to tell us about the 32 saloons and 18 bordellos of this old "Entertainment Capital of the Northwest". 180 pages ISBN 1-57502-427-6 pbk $16.95

A Field Guide to Historic The Dalles (c) 1997 by Keith F. May. Use this field guide to explore The Dalles' past as an Indian trading center, Methodist mission, Fort, site of a U.S. Mint, a rip roaring gold rush town and more. 178 pages ISBN 1-57502-446-2 pbk $15.95

Finding The Trail in Oregon: A Guide to Sites, Museums and Ruts on the Oregon Trail (c) 1996 by Keith F. May. Includes every public site of the Oregon Trail from Vale to Oregon City. 210 pages ISBN 1-57502-136-6 pbk $14.95

A Tour of Pendleton's Historic Homes (c) 1995 by Keith F. May The history and architecture of 29 Pendleton Homes. 70 pages ISBN 1-57502-090-4 pbk $9.95

TO ORDER ANY OF THESE TITLES:

Write the titles you wish to have, along with your mailing address, and enclose a check for the total of the books ordered plus $3.00 to cover shipping and handling to:

Drigh Sighed Publications
327 SE 1st Street, Suite 131
Pendleton, OR 97801

OR:

Write to the above address to obtain a free catalog of titles available and an order form.